OUT
OF THE
CORNER
OF MY EYE

OUT OF THE CORNER OF THE CORNER OF MY EYE

Living with Macular Degeneration

Nicolette Pernot Ringgold

AFB PRESS

American Foundation for the Blind

Printed in the United States of America.

Library of Congress Cataloging-in-Publication Data

Ringgold, Nicolette P., 1903–
  Out of the corner of my eye : living with macular degeneration / Nicolette Pernot Ringgold.—2nd ed.
      p. cm.
  Includes bibliographical references.
  ISBN 978-0-89128-831-2 (print : alk. paper)
  ISBN 978-0-89128-832-9 (ascii disk)
  1. Ringgold, Nicolette P., 1903—Health. 2. Retinal degeneration—Patients—Biography. 3. Older blind people—Biography. I. Title.
  RE661.D3R56 2007
  362.197'7350092—dc22
  [B]   2007030171

The findings and conclusions in the Foreword to this book are those of the author and do not necessarily represent the views of the Centers for Disease Control and Prevention.

Cover photo by Earl Dotter

The American Foundation for the Blind—the organization to which Helen Keller devoted her life—is a national nonprofit devoted to expanding the possibilities for people with vision loss.

It is the policy of the American Foundation for the Blind to use in the first printing of its books acid-free paper that meets the ANSI Z39.48 Standard. The infinity symbol that appears above indicates that the paper in this printing meets that standard.

Contents

Foreword

There are critical events in our lives that define who we are—events that test our courage, our ingenuity, and our will. For many people later in life, the loss of vision becomes that critical event.

Out of the Corner of My Eye is the story of Nicolette Pernot Ringgold. It is the story of one woman's encounter with macular degeneration, and it demonstrates her courage, her humor, and her capacity to deal with an extraordinarily difficult event. We must remember, however, that there are about six million older people in America who experience vision problems, and therefore, in many respects this story is one of six million stories that should be told.[1]

When *Out of the Corner of My Eye* was first published in 1991 by the American Foundation for the Blind, macular degeneration was the leading cause of vision loss in people age 60 and older. Today, it is still the leading cause of vision loss among older persons. About half of today's six million Americans with vision problems would be classified as having severe visual impairment (known as low vision) or blindness,[2] and about 1.75 million report having macular degeneration.[3]

---

[1] Crews, J. E., Jones, G. C., & Kim, J. H. (2006). Double jeopardy: The effects of comorbid conditions among older people with vision loss. *Journal of Visual Impairment & Blindness, 100,* 824–848.

[2] Eye Diseases Prevalence Research Group (2004). Causes and prevalence of visual impairment among adults in the United States. *Archives of Ophthalmology, 122,* 477–485.

Although our vision typically changes as we get older, aging in and of itself doesn't cause vision loss. For example, most of us become more sensitive to glare and may need increased illumination to read and do close work, but these normal changes are very different from diseases like macular degeneration and glaucoma, which are not an inevitable part of later life. However, certain eye conditions do appear with increased frequency among older persons. So, although advancing age does not cause vision loss, it does tend to predict it. For those aged 65 to 74, 13.8 percent experience some difficulty seeing. For those between the ages of 75 and 84, the prevalence increases to 19.3 percent, and for those aged 85 and over, the prevalence

---

[3] Eye Diseases Prevalence Research Group (2004). Prevalence of Age-Related Macular Degernation in the United States. *Archives of Ophthamology*, 122, 564–572.

is 29.9 percent.[4] For older people, therefore, compromised vision is not uncommon. But getting older brings many other life changes that demand their own often difficult adjustments, such as the loss of a spouse or dear friends and the development of various ailments, that can be further complicated by vision loss. Vision loss among older people is therefore serious business, not something to be dismissed as a normal part of aging.

In the face of what may seem like a daunting challenge, however, there is much that can be done in terms of vision rehabilitation services to teach skills and strategies for dealing with vision loss, improved

---

[4] Jones, G. C. (2007). Unpublished analysis of data from the National Center for Health Statistics. (1997–2004). National Health Interview Survey, Sample Adult Files. Hyattsville, MD: Centers for Disease Control and Prevention. Retrieved October 11, 2006, from www.cdc.gov/nchs/nhis.htm.

technologies to increase access to print and the environment, and simple ingenuity in responding to one's own circumstances (see the American Foundation for the Blind's Senior Site at www.afb.org/seniorsite for more information). In this book, Mrs. Ringgold recounts the help she received from her state's commission for the blind. There are rehabilitation services for older visually impaired people in every state, and many larger communities have private vision rehabilitation services with staff who can help with training, resources, and devices. Also, given what we know about health, it is important that people experiencing visual impairment make efforts to take care of their own health by eating right, getting sufficient exercise, and having frank discussions with physicians if sadness and the blues persist.

Nicolette Ringgold was a teacher and writer, and in *Out of the Corner of My Eye* she combines those two skills to share her own experiences with others. She was born in Paris, France, in 1903, was educated in France, and has a graduate degree in English from the University of Paris. After teaching French to non-French speakers in her own country, she was invited to teach at the Middlebury College Summer Language School in 1932, and she later joined the faculties of Wellesley College and the College of William and Mary.

Mrs. Ringgold published a number of articles on French phonetics, translated several works from the Dutch into French, and co-authored *Add Color to Your French* with her husband, Gordon B. Ringgold, who was a professor of French at the College of William and Mary. After she retired from teaching, she wrote a narrative account of her husband's experience with Alzheimer's disease to share with other caregivers. In 1982, at age 79, Mrs. Ringgold lost her central vision and became legally blind. She died in 2003 at the age of 99—her life spanning the 20th century. Given her talents as well as her lifelong interests in communicating with and reaching out helpfully to others, it is no surprise that her legacy lives on as she instructs us in her work, *Out of the Corner of My Eye.*

Mrs. Ringgold teaches us many important lessons in this book. It is rich in common sense and practical ideas for dealing with daily tasks, and she demonstrates a remarkable resourcefulness that can help almost anyone experiencing visual impairment—as well as those who care for and about older people who experience vision loss.

In a larger sense, though, Mrs. Ringgold offers us a model that teaches us all lessons about dealing with life's difficulties. She shows us that good humor and honesty go a long way in helping us face harsh events. She also demonstrates that persistence and a positive outlook are the qualities that can help get us through life.

Mrs. Ringgold's chronicle also asserts the integrity of the individual. Although the specific suggestions in this book may not be useful to everyone, in her unassuming way, their author most certainly champions the importance of taking risks and the willingness to adapt to and cope with dramatic life changes. By telling her story in the down-to-earth and practical way she does, she teaches us the best things about ourselves as human beings, for she helps us to recognize that our strength lies in our ability to solve problems and ultimately assert our will to shape events.

The issue of aging and blindness is not, of course, numbers, demographics, agencies, or policies; it is people—people who experience dramatic, intensely personal events that forever change their lives. Vision loss is an event that tests the resilience and capacity of older people, and it tests the families who love them.

Mrs. Ringgold teaches us strategies—an essential resilience—that enables individuals to cope. In her professional career, she taught people how to speak French and appreciate the language and literature of France. In her later years, she taught others about her husband's Alzheimer's disease, and in her retirement, she taught us once again, creating out of her own loss a work that reaches out to others who will find both strength and direction in this volume.

John E. Crews, D.P.A.
Lead Scientist
Disability and Health Team
National Center on Birth Defects and
Developmental Disabilities
Centers for Disease Control and Prevention
Atlanta, Georgia

Introduction

Macular degeneration is the leading cause of vision loss in people 60 years of age and older. Persons with macular degeneration do not become totally blind, but they lose their ability to see fine detail because of damage to the macula of the eye. It is the central portion of the retina that is responsible for the vision used to read, recognize faces, drive a car, and watch television. Although many people who develop vision loss may initially feel as though their lives will never be the same, there are many adaptations that can help them to keep doing the things that matter to them.

The story of Nicolette Ringgold, an 87-year old homemaker and retired college professor, is proof of this. *Out of the Corner of My Eye: Living with Macular Degeneration* is Mrs. Ringgold's account of experiencing vision loss at the age of 79. It is the story of how one woman dealt with losing a great deal of vision and confronting the frustrations brought about by this loss. It includes descriptions of predicaments in which persons with macular degeneration or other forms of vision loss may find themselves and the simple strategies that Mrs. Ringgold has used to adjust to them.

A good deal has changed for people with vision loss since Mrs. Ringgold wrote these words in 1991. Today, there are many more products available to assist people with vision loss, and technology, especially computers and the Internet, has made everything to do with reading, writing, and obtaining information significantly easier.

For example, there are portable electronic magnifiers that you can take with you to the store or restaurant; "talking" products such as calculators, scales, or even blood glucose monitors for diabetes that speak aloud the reading on the dial; and computer software that "reads" the contents of the computer's screen aloud.

We have chosen for the most part to leave Mrs. Ringgold's words alone so that she can still tell her inspiring story in her own voice. But, at the end of each chapter, we have provided some information on how things have changed and some of the newer techniques and products that are available. Much more detailed information is available elsewhere. The American Foundation for the Blind (AFB) has published other books, including *Aging and Vision Loss: A Handbook for Families* and *Making Life More Livable: Simple Adaptations for Living at Home After Vision Loss*, and AFB's Senior Site web site is available on the Internet (at www.afb.org/seniorsite) with a wealth of information. The Resources appendix at the end of this book can also guide you in finding the information that you need.

Working at AFB's Center on Vision Loss in Dallas gives us a fresh and personal look at the experiences that people are having in today's world with macular degeneration. Although much has changed since Mrs. Ringgold wrote this wonderful story; much has not. There have been advances in treatment for the wet (neovascular) type of macular degeneration, caused by the abnormal growth of blood vessels under the retina, which affects only about 10 to 15 percent of those with macular degeneration but causes 90 percent of all cases of vision loss from the disease. However, there are still no substantive treatments for the majority of people with the slower developing dry type of macular degeneration that causes deposits known as drusen to form on the retina—although studies suggest that nutritional supplements and eating antioxidant-rich foods such as fresh fruits, dark-green leafy vegetables, and at least one serving of fish per week may delay the onset or reduce the severity of dry AMD. Despite what we have learned, the number of people with the condition is increasing exponentially every year as the population ages. In many ways, therefore, *Out of the Corner of My Eye* is more relevant than ever.

Living with macular degeneration can be challenging and frustrating, as we hear from people who come into our Center on Vision Loss every day, searching for a magic solution to help them read again and do other important tasks. We don't have a magic bullet for them, but we do have information about help that is available, devices for people to try, and simple solutions—such as changes they can make in their home using color contrast and texture—that make a huge difference in their ability to function more independently. Most of the time when we show people what they are still able to do, they leave feeling more at peace and hopeful. Through this book, we want to offer the same kind of hope to people who may have been told, "There is nothing more we can do to help you."

Although not all the tips and strategies offered here may work for everyone, and each individual may need to experiment to find the techniques that work best for him or her, they demonstrate how simple adjustments can make a world of difference in allowing people to continue to function as independently as possible. Along the way, they also demonstrate how far good humor and persistence can take someone in affirming that yes, there is life—a good life—after vision loss. And that has not changed.

Through the publication of this very personal account, AFB hopes to provide people who have reduced vision with a perspective that makes the statement, "If she can do it, we all can!"

Out of the Corner of My Eye remains a personal and compelling story of someone who lived successfully with macular degeneration and who shares her struggles and her triumphs with people who are coping with the condition now. According to Esther Smith, board member and volunteer at the Center on Vision Loss, who at age 81 has had macular degeneration for 12 years, "The lesson we can learn from Mrs. Ringgold is to be adventuresome and to use trial and error to find out what works for you." Esther, who has worked with us to update this book, has been just as successful in coping with her vision loss in the 21st century as Mrs. Ringgold was in the 20th, and her insights about living with macular degeneration make this timeless story even more insightful.

Please share this book with others and let them know that there is hope and help available.

Priscilla Rogers, Ph.D.
National Independent Living Associate

Judy Scott, M.S.
Director
Center on Vision Loss
American Foundation for the Blind
Dallas, Texas

✧ 1 ✧
First Impressions

"Macula" is a pretty word the first time you hear it, but in "macular degeneration" it has quite another sound. The macula, the little spot on the retina used for looking at fine details, may deteriorate gradually or be destroyed all of a sudden. In either case macular degeneration portends unforeseen complications, drastic changes in one's life-style, and some extremely difficult adjustments.

When macular degeneration strikes, the blow can at first be staggering. Resentment, despondency, and even depression may come into play. Some will ask, "Why me?" Others will concentrate on one particular loss: "I can never read again"; "I can't drive"; "I've lost my independence"; "Good-bye travel." For still others, the realization often comes in small doses: "I can't see the expression on my husband's face." "I can't play anymore—I can't see the notes." "Are these shoes brown or black?" "What time is it?" "Who's that letter from?" But then one takes stock, assesses the possibilities, and begins to make small adjustments: "Let's put the short envelopes on the left, the long ones on the right—then I can feel them." "Will you set the stove? I'll fix an oven dinner." "I'll lock the door; I can feel the keyhole with my fingers."

After my abrupt loss of vision, a local volunteer group who knew my situation because we all live in a small town contacted the state commission for the blind on my behalf. A young man from the commission came to see what I could and could not do and assess what my circumstances and needs were and how the commission could best meet them. His visit was followed by one from a woman who inspected the premises, gave me advice about safety measures, and indicated improvements that should be made. She pointed out hazards and, most helpful of all, labeled several appliances with small pieces of rough tape, so that sight could be replaced by touch. For example, she put markers on the knobs of the kitchen stove and on the two settings of the washing machine that I use most—regular cycle and delicate wash—and also two markers on my sewing machine for three-eighths and five-eighths of an inch. She brought specialized catalogs and helped me select whatever items fitted my individual needs. She had all kinds of practical advice to offer, bolstering my confidence and morale. She followed up with telephone calls and subsequent visits, checking on my progress and further needs. The dedication and know-how of such specialists are invaluable in easing the transition from the sighted person one was to the visually impaired person one has become.

Nevertheless, no matter how competent and concerned they are, these specialists often remain outsiders. Many of them can see. They have not lived through the innumerable mishaps and frustrations that are the daily lot of anyone with macular degeneration. After eight years of no central vision and only fuzzy peripheral vision, I would like to share with you general rules, small discoveries (often triggered by mishaps), and possibilities from my experience as an insider.

My Case

This may be the place to introduce myself. I'm 87 years old, I'm a retired college professor, and I have been a housewife for many years. Mine was a case of sudden loss of vision. For several years the vision in my right eye had been bad. It was macular degeneration, but I didn't know its name. It didn't bother me much because my left eye was very good. I used bifocals for reading or close work, but not for driving. I did a lot of reading, was a good seamstress and knitter, and enjoyed canning and making jams and cookies. One morning I woke up with no clear vision at all. A hemorrhage had destroyed the macula in my left eye. Overnight I had become legally blind. It was impossible to read or drive.

However, the woman sent by the state commission made an appointment for me with a doctor who tested my eyes for reading. He found that with a 10X magnifier, held very close to my left eye and very close to the paper, I could read some print, letter by letter. I bought one of those 10X magnifiers. It has become absolutely indispensable to me and is my only link to the written word. It is the shape and size of a small flashlight and operates with two C-cell batteries. It can be used as is or with the light turned on.*

Still, the first few weeks of semiblindness—for semiblindness it is—are extremely difficult. You know there is a book on the table; you look at it, and it has disappeared. Someone talks to you, and all you see is a body without a head. You know there is an armchair, but what has happened to the cushion?

Before I describe some of the problems I encountered, and the ways I found to cope with them, I should say that your difficulties and your strategies—may be different. The only generalization I can make is, Do

---

* For updated information about products and techniques available today to help individuals live independently with macular degeneration, please see the section "Living with Macular Degeneration Today" at the end of each chapter.

what works for you with the vision you have, but be mindful of safety. There may be a period of frustration ahead, but I've found that sometimes it's less the specific strategy than one's attitude that can carry the day.

New Perceptions

With macular degeneration, the first realization you have to come to terms with—which can take quite a while—is that parts of your eye can't see but others can still see and that you have to use those parts in a different way than you did before.

Experiment for a few minutes with something on a table—a vase of flowers, for instance. Look at it in your usual way; it won't be there. Then, without moving your head, move your eyes upward, downward, to the left, and to the right, and see when the flowers appear. Practice with various targets, high and low. Of course you will use a different part of your eye when you look at the ceiling or at the floor. Though it takes practice and perseverance to achieve it, once this trick is mastered, half the battle is won. Later you will discover with amazement that only with a conscious effort could you go back to looking straight ahead.

✧ Eyeglasses

If you have macular degeneration, peripheral vision is your major asset. If you have other kinds of vision loss, your remaining vision will be of a different sort. In any event, you may want to experiment with the most effective ways of using the vision that remains. I have found that wearing eyeglasses limits my peripheral vision. My old eyeglasses help a little for writing, but in a general way my visual field is wider and freer without the restriction of the glasses.

✧ Bright Light

Be prepared for a paradox. Bright light is probably your best friend for close work; writing, preparing vegetables, dialing a phone number, plugging in an appliance—all these and similar activities will benefit from a good source of light. But looking into an illuminated area such as a patch of sunlight on the floor, coming from the dark into a well-lighted room, facing any kind of glare—on a windshield, on a piece of metal, on the white shirtfronts of the musicians on a stage—and sitting under the ceiling lights in any modern office may be uncomfortable, even painful, and may necessitate shading or even closing one's eyes. When no close looking is required, it is preferable to sit with one's back to the source of light.

✧ Depth Perception and Distances

The loss of central vision has an immediate effect on distance evaluation. Whether you are reaching for something, putting something down on a surface, or determining the position of one object in relation to another, you are in an atmosphere of insecurity. Depth perception has become unreliable. The branch of a bush right outside the window may seem like a rope 20 yards farther away. An insect may look like an airplane. The lettuce leaf on the plate is not where you thought it was, and your fork goes empty to your mouth. You reach for the pitcher of iced tea and clutch a handful of empty air—that is, if you're lucky! On the way to the pitcher your hand may have come into contact with a tall glass with a spoon sticking out of it, and another spill or breakage may have occurred.

The safest way to reach for something is to slide your hand lightly across the table or other surface until it reaches the desired object, which can then be grasped. A little groping may be involved, but there will be fewer accidents than if you had reached normally and moved your hand a few inches above the tabletop.

Being a passenger in an automobile can be a terrifying experience, especially for an ex-driver. You may feel that your driver is going to sideswipe every car on your right and that any car coming toward you is heading straight for you. It takes many miles of inner gasps, closed eyes, and mental fortitude to turn a person with macular degeneration into a relaxed passenger.

The loss of central vision also affects depth perception in walking. Somehow, one's balance is no longer as steady as before, and I believe it would be quite difficult to walk a straight line for more than a few yards. No device I know of can correct the depth-perception problem, but it does become less acute as time goes on, as one adjusts to it.

✧ Fallen Objects

Although people with macular degeneration may, like everyone else, drop things through carelessness, most frequently the cause will be lack of depth perception. For

the same reason, picking things up becomes a difficult operation. If you're lucky,
you may have seen the object fall or heard
it come into contact with the linoleum, the
rug, or the wooden floor. Sweep the area
with your eye, up and down, right and left;
you will probably locate the dropped object. If not, a brush or broom may bring it
into sight. Looking toward the ten o'clock
or two o'clock position will usually keep it
in your field of vision. It may take several
tries for your hand to coordinate with your
eye and manage to get hold of the object.
It pays to practice a little, first with a penny,
then with a tiny scrap of paper, a grain of
rice, an apple-seed, or a pin. This skill will
also help when you have to wipe spills off
the floor. A small challenge: Try to pick up
an ice cube that has fallen to the floor.

Sometimes you feel very foolish. Have you
ever tried to pick up a flower that is part of
the pattern in the rug or to pick up a patch

of sunlight from the floor? I have, more than once.

✧ Recognition

Your degree of success in recognizing people may vary according to your degree of disability or your feeling for form. I can offer only my own experience and solutions. They may not be yours.

Faces are a blur, even my own. When I look in a mirror, I see two dark spots for the eyes, a vague contour for the face, and a white mass (the hair) above. When I look at other people, I see only a vague outline, eyeglasses or their absence, and hair. No features, no expression. When people come up to me, I may recognize them by their voices, but often I have to ask the very awkward question, "Who are you?" Those who remember my difficulty will start by saying, "I'm so-and-so," and we can go on from there.

Yet, despite the limitations, some signs facilitate recognition. Here contrasts play a definite role. Silhouettes stand out against a background; they show whether people are tall or short, thin or fat; they show how people walk, how they use their arms, what their posture is, and the shape of their heads. I realized that the outline of the hair can be very revealing. During visits to friends in hospitals and nursing homes, the nurses all wore uniforms. I sometimes couldn't tell if their skin was black or white, but I recognized one by her wide hips, another by her way of scurrying around, and another by her regal posture. Most of all I recognized them by their hairdos, which gave a distinctive shape to their heads and were clearly defined against a background. In the beginning I would have to ask, "Are you Susan?" "Are you Teresa?" But after a while I could tell; no faces yet, but recognition.

At a social gathering, at a club meeting, after a concert, I can recognize some

14

friends but not acquaintances. I am not familiar enough with their silhouettes. And in a crowd, my companion will have to find me; I can't find my companion. When someone takes me to a store, I make a mental picture of what the person is wearing—a raincoat, a striped shirt, a black sweater, plaid slacks—so that I can recognize my escort in the crowded aisles.

Vital Assets

Someone with macular degeneration still has three main assets. The first and most important is peripheral vision. It is not sharp; in fact, it is rather fuzzy, but it does allow us to have a general knowledge of our environment and to get around fairly confidently in a world that has lost most of its finer points. The second is perception of motion. I see a dark mass on the lawn; is it a bird, a big leaf, or a squirrel? Only its motion will give me an answer.

The third big asset is the ability to see contrasts. At this point I would like to mention
a very simple device for which I have discovered many uses: a plain square of rigid
cardboard, preferably black. Though mine
is the back of an old calendar, it is such
a necessary part of daily life that I would
almost call it an appliance. It serves two
purposes. The first one is as a support for
reading material. When you want to read a
letter, circular, or newspaper clipping, you
may find that it is crumpled or has creases
or that it bends over in your hand. But
your magnifier, if you use one, requires a
smooth surface for reading. If you put the
cardboard behind your reading material as
a support, the paper stays smooth and you
can use your magnifier.

The second purpose of the cardboard
is much more important: It provides a
background against which you can create
contrasts. The fact that your cardboard is

black means that anything you place on it, of any color whatsoever (except black itself and other very dark colors such as navy blue), will stand out and be visible.

Contrasts

The ability to see contrasts is mostly unconscious. Once you are aware of it, however, it can be cultivated and expanded; its benefits will show in every phase of daily life. Using a black cardboard is a good beginning. It is invaluable when you want to write something—shopping list, short note, telephone message, reminder to yourself. The edges of the paper stand out clearly. The cardboard will show the outline of an envelope so that half of someone's address doesn't get written on the tablecloth. It also helps in situating the stamp and a return-address sticker in their proper corners. It serves as a foil for such elusive articles as pens, buttons, paper clips, and jewelry. You can sort coins on it, draw a line along its edge, contrast shapes, and contrast colors. In short, it is a very useful, very inexpensive gadget.

Contrasts may be made with almost anything, even between distant objects. Often a distant background will do. You don't know whether the tulips in your vase are faded or not. Hold up the bouquet against the distant background of a dark door. You will see the outline of the flowers much more clearly. If your indispensable magnifier has a dark handle and has disappeared, you may have left it on a dark surface somewhere. It would stand out on a light one, or if you wound light-colored tape around the handle. If you buy a ballpoint pen, choose one with colors whose contrast will make it easier to find than a black one. When you're sewing, use pins with dark heads on light-colored material and yellow- and white-headed pins on dark material, to provide a contrast. The same for basting threads: dark on light, light on dark. Take advantage of angles to create contrasts. Pens, pencils, needles, crochet hooks, and knitting needles are often difficult to locate because they blend well with their environment. If you put them down at an angle to whatever design or shape they rest on, you will retrieve them more easily. Sometimes you will find that the contrast is in the texture: rough or smooth pattern; right side or wrong side; stiff or supple material.

Black, of course, is the best color for contrast, black and yellow or black and white the best combination. That is one reason why black-and-white television is preferable to color television and why printing in light colors—light blue on white or red on pink paper—is impossible to read.

✦ Living with Macular ✦ Degeneration Today

"Low vision" is the term used today for the type of vision Mrs. Ringgold describes—as well as any vision loss that seriously interferes with everyday activities. Low vision specialists—optometrists or ophthalmologists—evaluate people with low vision and prescribe devices, such as magnifiers, that help them use their remaining vision. The workers from the state commission for the blind who came to visit Mrs. Ringgold to help her make changes to her home and master the skills necessary to carry out routine daily tasks are known today as "vision rehabilitation therapists" (or sometimes rehabilitation teachers). Every state has an agency for the blind or a department of rehabilitation that is in charge of providing services to adults who have low vision or are blind, either directly through that department or through local vision rehabilitation agencies. The Resources section at the end of this book gives information on how to locate these agencies and these and other services in your community.

The technique Mrs. Ringgold describes for using a different part of your eye to view objects in front of you is known as "eccentric viewing"; more on the subject can be found on the Senior Site web page of the American Foundation for the Blind (AFB at afb.org/seniorsite).

The principles and coping skills described by Mrs. Ringgold—using contrast, peripheral (or side) vision, texture, labeling and marking, good lighting without glare, and motion—remain the same. Chapter 2 contains more information on how to manage everyday activities, and many more techniques, strategies, and suggestions are available on AFB's Senior Site web page and in the books listed in the Resources section of this book.

In contrast to the basic principles, many of the devices and technology that are now available to help people with macular degeneration manage everyday tasks successfully have changed and evolved considerably since Mrs. Ringgold wrote in 1991. To take just a few examples, in addition to the 10x magnifier Mrs. Ringgold describes, today there are portable magnifying systems available that will magnify many more times and can still be slipped into a pocket or purse. Esther Smith says, "The portable magnifier has given me freedom away from home to read menus in restaurants and prices in the grocery store." Today's technology has made "talking" devices—tools or appliances that simulate speech—easily available. Some examples are talking clocks and watches, talking weight scales, talking thermometers, talking glucometers for people with diabetes, and talking devices that read aloud the prescription on medication labels. Lighting is another key issue for people with low vision—the right lighting can make all the difference in what you can see. Using appropriate task lighting to read, knit or sew, or work in the kitchen is critical. Natural daylight bulbs, both incandescent and fluorescent, are now available in local stores. These and many other special products and devices are available from the specialty catalogs listed in the Resources section.

Mrs. Ringgold describes her own abilities to recognize other people—friends and distant acquaintances. But, as Esther Smith notes, "In many cases people may experience a greater loss of recognition than Mrs. Ringgold explains. I cannot see heads at all, for example, from my central vision." She finds that using eccentric vision helps with recognition. Paying attention to voices and unique speech patterns also helps. Esther notes that when it comes to awkward situations, she finds "the best thing to do is to tell people up front that I may not recognize them and to let me know who they are. I've had to learn the hard way. Some people have thought I was snooty when I didn't say hello to them." There is a video with simulations of what the world looks like to people with different vision conditions on AFB's Senior Site that may be useful for explaining to family members and others what you are able to see.

Remember that everyone's vision is different. For example, Esther Smith prefers color television, while Mrs. Ringgold found she saw better with black and white. As Esther noted in the Introduction to this book, "The lesson we can learn from Mrs. Ringgold is to be adventuresome and use trial and error to find out what works for you."

✧ 2 ✧
At Home:
How to Manage

When your vision has been reduced, managing to do the things you did before and preventing accidents or mishaps become two central concerns. Becoming organized, proceeding carefully, and being persistent will pay great dividends.

Getting Organized

Busy people with unimpaired vision can usually put their hands without hesitation on whatever they need around the house. Not so those with impaired vision. They may come home, put their keys on the table, hang up their coats, change their clothes, and then think: "Where did I put my keys?" They don't see them but have to find them. Before hanging up their coats, they should have put the keys away where they usually keep them, in a pocket, purse, or other special place. Another scenario: "Let's have a cup of tea. Where did the sugar go? Now, where did I use it last? For the applesauce I made last night. Here it is on the stove!" That sugar should have been put back last night on the tray where it belongs. Or: "What did I do with the check from the bank? I thought I put it on the desk. It's not on the table. It's not with the letters. Oh, maybe under the newspaper. Yes! Here it is." That check should have been put in the desk drawer. The moral: Put things where they belong as soon as you have finished with them. It will save a lot of time and trouble. "A place for everything and everything in its place"—still a good motto for home and workshop—can be the key to survival to a person with low vision.

Putting things away after you use them not only helps you find them again, it helps you avoid clutter and unexpected encounters that can lead to accidents. Do not put any object on the floor. Don't leave shoes around. Indoors you don't usually walk with your eyes looking at the floor, so you're apt to stumble over an obstacle. Also beware of electrical cords. If you carry a lamp, a fan, or the toaster from one place to another, be sure to gather the cord in your hand so that it doesn't trail on the floor where your foot might get caught in it. And don't ever leave anything on the stairs. The stairs are the most dangerous part of the house, and anything left on them only adds to the danger.

In the Kitchen

Mishaps in the kitchen are fairly common events for everyone, whether visually impaired or not. We all handle many things in the kitchen, and the occasions for trouble are numerous. When my vision was re-duced, I found spilling—over and over again—to be the most constant difficulty. This was the result of not being able to see clearly and having faulty depth perception. It is a frustrating situation, and sometimes the best remedies are patience and a roll of absorbent paper towels. A principle to remember in the kitchen is never to put anything tall in front of something low—not on the counter, not on the table, and not when you stack the dishes. Failure to observe this rule is the surest way to spill-ing and breaking. Still, there are ways of avoiding spills and working comfortably in the kitchen that are based on the use of color contrast, good organization and planning, and methods of doing things based on your sense of touch.

✧ Handles

Saucepans, pots, and frying pans on the stove require special attention. Their han-dles should always be turned toward the back. If they are not, any unguarded movement may upset them and cause tragedy. The danger of burns is very great: Even jostling a wooden spoon or a large fork may upset a pan. Turning all handles and utensils to the back is an elementary rule in households with children or visually impaired persons. It should be a rule in every household.

✧ Drinking Glasses

Anything transparent or made of glass might as well not exist for someone with macular degeneration, and drinking glasses are a special hazard. It pays to invest in a set of glasses with heavy bottoms and ribbing, or heavy bottoms and colored, eye-catching designs. Placing a coaster under a glass may also make the glass more visible.

✧ Pouring

Pouring takes a lot of skill. By putting a finger tip lightly on the rim of your glass, you will help direct your pouring hand to the proper position. You may want to try using a funnel to fill glasses or cups, but this is a tricky, unstable method whose success depends on a good degree of vision and dexterity. Take advantage of color contrasts. Dark-colored liquids show up better in pots or containers that have light-colored inside surfaces, and light-colored liquids show up better against dark surfaces. If you are a coffee drinker, an investment you might consider is a set of coffee cups or mugs with insides that are light in color, so you can see the level of coffee when you pour it, and mugs that are not white inside, so you can tell the level of the milk. Soups or other liquids, such as sauces, are best transferred from a saucepan into a bowl or dish with a ladle.

✧ Bottles

Be sure to close immediately any bottle you have finished using. In my experience, vanilla and salad dressing bottles can be especially unstable. If you leave a bottle open, the slightest motion of your hand can send the contents spilling out over the countertop or onto the floor.

✧ Knives

Some knives can be recognized by the color or shape of their handles. With others the cutting edge of the blade is not always easy to find. By making a notch or putting a small piece of tape at the place where your thumb should be, you will know which side to avoid with your fingers.

✧ Cooking

There is no reason why a person with impaired vision cannot cook. The process will be slower, there will be accidents, and some elegant touches may be missing, but meals can be just as good as before. I have found that cooking, baking, canning, and preserving are all within my scope as a low vision person when I work in familiar surroundings. In a strange kitchen I believe it would be better to abstain.

At the Table

Serving may present quite a challenge for the visually impaired host or hostess. "There's many a slip twixt cup and lip" can apply just as well to dish and plate. One solution is to do the carving and serving in the kitchen and have the filled plates ready for the guests when they come to the table. But that does away with the groaning board and the ceremonial carving of the turkey or roast at Thanksgiving or other holiday feasts. Still, one can follow the European custom of passing the dishes and having the guests help themselves. But what of the visually impaired guest? He or she will have the same difficulty as the host or hostess in transferring the food from the dish to the plate and may have to turn to a sighted neighbor for assistance during the meal.

Once the food is served, new problems arise. Where is the meat? Does it have to be cut? Where are the vegetables? What are they? A color contrast between the plate and the food or between the different kinds of food may provide a clue. Carrots, spinach, and ham are a happy combination. But suppose you are faced with a main course consisting of creamed chicken, potatoes, and cauliflower. With three white foods, every forkful will prove a surprise. Sometimes knowing that the meat is at six o'clock, with one vegetable at two and the other at eleven o'clock, eases the problem. In any case, some maneuvering may be necessary to empty one's plate without accident. The last morsels are especially difficult to capture, and the knife may have to be brought into action to push the food onto the fork. (Although not officially "sanctioned," the use of a small spoon would certainly help at times like these.)

Some items can prove particularly awkward, for example, lettuce and meat on the bone. When they are not torn into small pieces before they are served, lettuce leaves are too large and difficult to cut. Meat like lamb chops and chicken legs and breasts require skill with knife and fork, unless, of course, fingers are considered acceptable utensils. When I eat out, I steer clear of foods that require too much skill with utensils.

When being handed a cup, a plate, or a dish, one cannot always gauge the weight of the object. It is safer to extend both hands to receive it. This may look a little clumsy, but it may avoid dropping or spilling.

In the Bathroom

The shiny, slippery surfaces found in bathrooms present many dangers to people with vision loss, but I haven't had great difficulties in this area—perhaps because I have a stall shower and no bathtub. The presence of a tub calls for safety measures as well as increased caution.

I have had to make adjustments with smaller items, however. For example, I now immediately close shampoo bottles after use in case they tip over. When buying toothpaste, I buy the colored kind. It enables you to tell how much you put on your toothbrush. Some caps on toothpaste tubes used to be red, but most were white and had a way of disappearing when you put them down on the sink. Now manufacturers have come up with flip-top tubes, much appreciated by low vision people.

Steps and Stairs

To a person who cannot see well, steps and stairs are a nightmare. Whenever possible, the first safety measure should be to install banisters or railings along any stairs that do not already have this feature, to provide support for the person going up or down and reduce the risk of a slip or fall. Going up is not too bad; a slight shadow indicates the edge of each step. But going down there is no shadow, and the edge of the step blends with whatever is beneath. You can't tell where the step ends. A good safety device is a narrow yellow or white strip painted on or pasted to the flat edge of each step so that a person going down can tell where the step ends. Someone going up should automatically count steps in order to know how many there will be coming down. Many an accident testifies to the fact that there was one more step going down. When dealing with stairs, one should grip the banister firmly and feel for the steps carefully with one's foot.

The doorways of many stores are not flush with the sidewalk. When you open the door to enter, you may find a very shallow step up. You may not even be conscious of this step because it is at the same level as the bottom of the door, but beware! When you leave, it will have become a step down, just deep enough to trip you. Some stores have a kind of wide apron between the door and the sidewalk or the street, with a definite step at the end of the apron. In two instances I have pointed out the danger to the manager, and the next time I went to the store, the apron had a yellow edging. One big hazard gone!

When going down unfamiliar steps that have no markings, proceed slowly and with caution. The recommended method for exploring where the edge of a stair is involves using the toe of one foot. Whatever you do, it is important to be careful to maintain your balance. I test the depth of the first stair by tapping my heel lightly against the riser of the stair. When I'm sure of the stair's depth, position, and distance, I put my foot down and go down from there. I use the same procedure to test a curb.

Television

People who rely on television for news and entertainment may perceive the loss of central vision as a near catastrophe. The screen may look to them like a blur of brilliant colors without contours or shapes but with twirling patterns and constant flashes of bright light that can hurt their eyes; they may hear only disembodied voices and cryptic announcements bereft of their visual explanations. No human faces or figures; no intriguing animal behavior; no Miss America; no boxing or football or diving competitions or sports of any kind; no news; no plays, movies, or sitcoms; no late-late show; and no lovers walking into the sunset.

However, there is a possibility. (It worked for me; I don't know whether it will for others.) During one winter, I happened to turn on the TV during the Olympics and, as usual, the bottom of the screen was a white blur with a few objects moving on it. I put on dark glasses and immediately recognized that the small objects were skiers. I could not see any details but could see their graceful movements on the ski slopes. Some time later, quite by chance, I tried to get the news on a black-and-white TV and saw the announcer appear. I realized that black-and-white TV, by eliminating the bright flashes of color TV, provided me with location (a house, a room, a basketball court), with human figures (especially when moving), with faces in close-ups. I cannot see the tournament score printed on the screen, but I can see the bent back of the golfer trying to putt. If your experience is the same as mine, even a small black-and-white TV might be a good investment.

I still prefer to get the news on the radio. The voices are clearer and the announcers know that their audience is all ears, not all eyes. They interpret their material accordingly.

Reading, Writing, and Communicating

Vision plays a large part in activities like reading and writing. When your vision becomes impaired, changes in these activities are inevitable. I now find that words typewritten all in capital letters are awfully difficult to read. The characters are all the same height and close together, and the contrast is practically nil. I discovered that the word POLICE typed in all capital letters could just as well be POLITE and that EXECUTIVE could be EXCLUSIVE. Printed words with rounded letters and space around them are not such a problem, and words with lowercase letters are another story. *Washington* (for example) with lower-case letters has a capital *W* and an *h*, a *g*, and a *t* that stand out from the rest of the letters and make the word recognizable. *Birthday* in lowercase has the *b, t, h,* and *d* above and the *y* below the other letters, which immediately gives the word its character. This is especially important for names and addresses. My address book is now typed on index cards. My magnifier picks up typing much more clearly than it does handwriting. Typing is more uniform, has no curlicues or flourishes. It takes up less space for the magnifier to travel over, and the contrast is often better.

✧ The Written Word

When it comes to producing readable material, lucky the person who learned to type before becoming visually impaired. The ability to type makes communications of all kinds much easier, whether they be personal messages, business transactions, or lists. When you can't see what your pen puts down, you may encounter unexpected pitfalls. To me, double *o's, e's, m*'s, and *n*'s (two legs or three?) are real hazards. *Good* and *soon* turn out to have three *o*'s more often than two. One line gets written on top of another, so that neither one is legible.

Dotting *i*'s and crossing *t*'s can be a problem, too. Two options are available. If you write the whole word and then come back to dot your *i*'s and cross your *t*'s, the dot for the *i* may float somewhere above a *g*, and the stroke for the *t* may look like underlining for the word above. Or, if you dot your *i*'s and cross your *t*'s as they come along, your words will end up chopped into little pieces. Either way will be a little awkward to decipher.

After more than eight years of being severely visually impaired, I find that my handwriting has deteriorated and is getting more and more difficult for others to read. The lines slope down; letters are omitted, words truncated. I can type, but not well. Hitting a key one space to the left or to the right can produce a chain re-action, and a word like *this* can become *yjod* or *rgua*. But mistakes are generally confined to *i* for *o* or *v* for *c*—simple sub-stitutions of letters anyone with any imagi-nation can correct.

Any important letter or paper of which a copy has to be kept begins with, "Please excuse the mistypings; I am blind." And after that I do the best I can, since I can neither erase, cross out, nor correct. For chatty letters to family or friends, the type-writer, by all means; for personal notes, the most careful handwriting possible.

✧ Other Difficulties and Solutions
Prolonged absence from the written word may produce another victim—spelling. Even the best speller may lose confidence (". . . *ent* or . . . *ant*?" "*y* or *i*?" "Double *t* or single?"). What to do when you can't look up the word in a dictionary? Enlist

the help of a friend, as you do when you need to have your weight read or a form filled out.

The state commission for the blind provided me with several templates to help with handwriting problems. All are black for contrast. One is a small rectangle, slightly smaller than an audiocassette, with a slot for a signature. The other is a page-size template with slots for horizontal lines that you can feel with your hand. An inch before the end of each line there is a small protuberance warning that there is room left for only a short word. This template prevents overlapping. A third template is meant for a checkbook. It is custom made to fit your particular checks. It has slots for the date, the amount in both numbers and words, the payee, and the signature.

My bank had another excellent solution: a slightly larger check with bold black lines that can be felt by the fingers. Instead of writing slanting down or putting the payee where the amount should be, I now have "everything in its place" and beautiful horizontal writing.

✧ The Telephone

My 87-year-old fingertips are not very sensitive, and I have trouble with a Touch-tone telephone. I have an old-fashioned rotary telephone, which I find much easier to use. I have a small piece of string tied to number 6, which gives me 5, 6, and 7. For 1, 2, and 3 and 8, 9, and 0, I use one, two, or three fingers in the holes. That leaves only the number 4 unaccounted for, and that one is easy to reach from 6 or even from 1.

By the way, do you know that in many places there are free telephone numbers for directory assistance, weather reports, and the time of day? If you use a rotary telephone (for which you can't program in common numbers that you call), you may want to memorize them, together with those of your doctor and the police and fire departments. Many towns also have other forms of directory assistance and telephone services and devices available for elderly and disabled people.

✧ Audiocassettes

Another channel of communication is open to us: cassettes. They can fill the same role as letters, but how much richer and more personal they are! They carry not only the message but the actual voice, the inflections, the shades of meaning that the same words in written form would not convey. They record conversations, performances, events of all kinds in a direct and lively way no letter can achieve. My sister lives in Paris. Her frequent cassettes to me are regular family chronicles, but they also let me share directly in the activities around her. She reads me articles from magazines and newspapers and records a radio interview; her grandchildren perform on piano and cello; she tells of the latest architectural marvel being constructed; she tapes the ceremony of my niece's wedding, sings a song from our childhood with a line missing that I am supposed to supply, opens a window to let me hear the sounds of a patriotic parade going by in the street, reads me part of the catalog of an exposition she recently visited, and, in passing, mentions the price of brussels sprouts and pork chops.

The oral message of cassettes can be repeated over and over again without the need for a reader. Since the visual for us has mostly been replaced by the oral, cassettes provide a direct line to the visual world through a medium with which we are familiar and which is readily available to us.

✧ Talking Books

The greatest boon of all for persons with macular degeneration is a program originating from the National Library Service for the Blind and Physically Handicapped, which is part of the Library of Congress in Washington, DC. The program is absolutely free and provides complete recorded books, called Talking Books. Some are read by men, others by women.

To join the program all you have to do is fill out an application at any local library or library for the blind. You will first receive a form asking you to check the categories of books you are interested in—travel, romance, westerns, biographies, mysteries, science fiction, religion, economics, and so on.

You will also receive a special cassette player. Inside is a cassette, one side in English and one in Spanish, with all the information you need to work the machine, which runs on electricity or batteries. The batteries are in the machine, and the instructions tell you how to recharge them. The machine will play aloud, but you can ask for earphones. I find the sound much clearer with earphones.

The Talking Book cassettes are recorded at a speed different from that of commercial cassettes. Both kinds can be used on the Talking Book player because it has a setting for each speed, but if you try a Talking Book cassette on a regular player, you will get nothing but gibberish.

Together with your machine you will receive one or two cassettes from the categories you selected. Every two months you will be sent a catalog listing the latest cassettes for adults and children, as well as some magazines and a few books in foreign languages. You may request that the catalog be sent to you in large print or on a disk or cassette. The catalog gives a short description of each book. You list the books you select and send the list to the nearest library for the blind or call in your choices.

The library sends you the books one or two at a time. The cassettes come addressed to you in green mailing boxes delivered by the postal service. When you have finished reading a book, put the cassettes back in the green box, fasten it, and turn over the address card. The name and address of the library that sent you the book are printed on the other side. All you have to do to return the cassettes is to hand the green box to your mail carrier or drop it in the nearest mailbox. No postage is needed. The whole procedure is simple and extremely well organized. To ensure a steady flow of books, it is recommended that you return the books promptly.

The most marvelous feature of the program is the quality of the narrators. They are absolutely fantastic. If your selection is a play, they will give you the various characters in different voices. An Irish story will have an Irish lilt. They can imitate any number of accents—British, southern, Jewish,

Russian, Italian, French, German. They make the books come completely alive, and you find yourself forgetting that you are listening; instead, you have a feeling that you are reading normally. I cannot recommend the program enough. For many people, especially the recently visually impaired, it is a real lifesaver.

Sewing, Knitting, and Crocheting

Sewing is a frustrating experience. The first hurdle is threading the needle. Fortunately, mail order companies sell a small gadget that does the job very neatly. You put the needle (eye down) into a small funnel, put the thread in a groove while you press a little lever, catch the thread, and pull out a threaded needle.

Suppose you want to do such a simple thing as putting up a hem, and you need to use a measuring tape. Have one ready that your fingers can read. I have one with a staple at every inch marking and two staples at the 12-, 24-, and 36-inch markings. Others have small metal holes at every inch and half-inch so you can feel the lengths and widths measured.

Use pins with colored and extra-large heads. They show up well on the material and are easier to take out, and to pick up if you drop them. For basting, use a double thread. It cannot slip out of the needle.

When it comes to the sewing itself, be prepared for a disappointment. Small, neat stitches are just about impossible. Do you need to sew on a button? Allow 15 minutes for a job that used to take 3 or 4. If you should decide to be ambitious and make a garment, as you used to do so easily, I hope you will remember how to thread your machine and have one of those fine wire loops to pull the thread through the eye of the needle. This is where the three-eighths-inch and five-eighths inch markers put on by the woman from the state commission come into their own for me. They indicate the edge of the fabric and should keep you on the straight and narrow.

I used to do a lot of knitting. Now, although I know it can be done, I can't count stitches with my fingers. If I drop a stitch, I can't retrieve it. The results of my efforts couldn't pass muster, so I gave it up. For brave souls or knitters more skillful than I, brightly colored needles may be helpful.

I had better luck with crocheting, however. I tried any number of stitches and finally discovered one I could use with confidence. It consists of a single stitch, a one and one-half stitch (that is, yarn over, pick up a loop, and go through all three loops at one time), then a chain stitch, and repeat. On the way back make your cluster in the opening left by the chain stitch in the preceding row. Your other hand can find the place and guide you. The clusters are easy to count and will make afghans, scarves, or anything you can think of.

Useful Devices

A great number of helpful low vision products are available through specialized catalogs. Consultation with a specialist and getting advice on the most useful items for you are of great value. Since people's vision differs so much, what different people will find helpful will differ too, but in my own experience I've found certain items invaluable.

✧ Clocks

Although one can get the time of day by dialing the appropriate telephone number, it is of great convenience to have a striking clock. It need not be elaborate as long as it strikes the hour and half hour. It will regulate and simplify the daily routine and, if it is not electric, stand by you in case of a power outage.

I was given a talking clock, and I am enjoying it very much, especially during sleepless nights. But it is a luxury, not a necessity. It has a number of push buttons. One will tell you in a hearty baritone, "The time is 3:13 A.M." There is a button for "his" alarm, another for "hers." There's one for snooze, another for a louder voice. Its main disadvantage is that the whole system goes back to 12:00 A.M. as the time if there is the slightest interruption in power. So, an ordinary striking clock may be preferable, unless you forget to wind it.

✧ Watches

Watches for blind people have a cover that can be opened and no crystal, so your fingers can feel the position of the hands on the dial. I tried one and found it rather cumbersome. After some searching,

I discovered a regular Timex watch with a white face and black hands, which had enough contrast so I could see the time. It also has a second hand that is sometimes confusing, but on the whole the watch is quite satisfactory. Other brands of watches with large faces and high contrast may also prove useful for you.

✧ Thermometers

I have a medical thermometer made for blind people. It consists of a metal rod at the end of which is a small white dial. As with the watch for blind persons, there is no crystal to cover it. The figures (94, 96, 98, 100, 102, 104, 106) are printed in black. A small red hand points to 98.6; a small black one indicates the patient's temperature. Both hands can be felt with one's fingers. The long stem of the thermometer attached to the dial is inserted under the tongue. Before removing it, one depresses a button that locks in the temperature. It can then be read either by the fingers or visually, using a magnifier. Pulling out the button will make the thermometer operable again.

In regard to the weather outdoors, if you are interested in knowing the specific temperature, you may want to buy an outside thermometer that will give you precise information. I have one mounted just outside a window. It is the size of a dinner plate and has bold black markings for both Fahrenheit and centigrade temperatures. The position of the black hand makes it very easy to read.

✧ Mirror

An ordinary mirror will give you a reflection but usually a very imperfect one. You may see the outline of your face or recognize where your mouth and your eyes are, but not much more. If you use cosmetics, applying makeup becomes a hazardous enterprise. There is, however, a product on the market that I believe might solve the difficulty. It is a powerful magnifying mirror, about 6 inches square, with strong illumination provided by four AA batteries. It enables you to see your face much better.

✧ Cane

Another aid is a collapsible cane that is small enough to fit in a woman's purse. It can be assembled by a flick of the wrist. It is not meant for support but, when extended, helps a great deal in traffic situations. My cane is used to indicate that I'm visually impaired, but there is a variety of long canes that people can learn to use to assist them in getting around and avoiding danger. I am lucky enough to be able to go walking by myself. I use the cane only when I have to cross a busy street, not by sweeping the road with it, as special training can teach you to do, but by holding it up at an angle in front of me. Most motorists, but not all, will give the little old lady the right of way. It still pays to be very careful.

When visiting in France I carried the French emblem of visual impairment, a white round cane, hooked over my arm. People were very considerate, helping me in and out of buses, and on the crowded streets they made a point of giving me elbow room. Even others reaped the benefits—my daughter said she was jostled much less when I accompanied her to the marketplace.

✦ Living with Macular ✦ Degeneration Today

Organization—having a designated place for everything in your home and putting objects away as soon as you finish using them—is still one of the key principles for living independently with low vision. However, there are a number of devices and technologies on the market to which Mrs. Ringgold did not have access that can help with coping with a number of everyday tasks. Most of the products mentioned here are available from the specialty catalogs listed in the Resources section. Additional tips and strategies are found on AFB's Senior Site web site and in its book *Making Life More Livable*, particularly in regard to making sure that getting around your home is as safe and easy as possible.

In the kitchen, in addition to Mrs. Ringgold's helpful hints, try large-print cookbooks that are now easily available. Mark frequently used settings on the stove and microwave with tactile or brightly colored products that you can feel or see, such as bump dots or Hi-Marks. For pouring, try an electronic liquid-level indicator that beeps when you get close to the top—or, if fixing a cold drink for yourself, place your finger just inside the cup or glass and pour the liquid until it touches your finger. Different kinds of labels are available to help identify cans, bottles, and other items.

For cutting, there are the pivot knife (which is anchored securely to the cutting board), the rocker knife, and slicers for slicing to-matoes. Dark or light cutting boards that contrast well with the food are useful as well. A variety of products are available for measuring ingredients, such as measuring cups and spoons with braille or large-print numbers. And audible, tactile, and large-print kitchen timers are available as well.

Using color contrast to make objects more visible is an important principle in every room of the house, but it is especially helpful for the dangerous areas that Mrs. Ringgold points out, such as the bathroom and stairs. Use towels and other products that contrast with the bathroom walls. Paint banisters and the edges of steps with a contrasting color as well.

For television watching, large-button and talking remote controls are commer-cially available, and the Resources section explains how to find programs, as well as movies, that have been described for visually impaired viewers. Alternatives to the TV and newspapers, in addition to regular radio programs, include radio reading services and the NFB Newsline.

Today the computer has become a great way to communicate, through both word processing and e-mail. Using a computer and printer instead of a typewriter makes it easy to produce your own large-print documents, and you can find errors through spell check and the automatic word correction features of some programs. Special software can be used to magnify the images on the screen and to read aloud the text. And, although cassettes are rarely used, there are even more ways today to share audio recordings when you want to hear someone's voice

Options for reading have also increased. The Talking Book program of the Library of

Congress is still a lifeline for many people who can't read print, although it is phasing out books on cassette in favor of digital formats. Today you can register online. Many books are available in audio format on commercial CDs as well. Electronic books also now exist in formats that can be played on a different types of commercial players, as well as on devices designed especially for persons with vision loss, with many available on the Internet (see the Resources section). In addition, electronic magnifiers can help a great deal in reading regular print; they come in portable versions that you can carry with you or as large as a 20-inch television set and are available in black and white and color. Scanners are also available that can read aloud the text of typewritten letters, bills, and books.

The principles of dialing a telephone haven't changed that much since Mrs. Ringgold described them, even though rotary phones are hard to find today. When using a pushbutton telephone, rest your fingers on the middle row of buttons—the 4, 5, and 6—then move up and down a row to find the other keys. The "5" key can be marked with a bump dot to help orient oneself to the keypad, if it is not already marked. Large-button telephones are commercially available, and today's telephones can also be programmed for one-button dialing of selected numbers. Cell phones come with programmed voice dialing, and a few come with large key pads.

There have also been many advances in watches and clocks. Large-numeral watches and talking watches are now available. To avoid the problem of resetting clocks after a power interruption, atomic clocks are available that reset the time automatically, and some talking clocks come with backup batteries. Talking and large-numeral thermometers are now readily available and much easier to use than the thermometer Mrs. Ringgold used. Talking outdoor thermometers are available as well. All these products and resources for people with vision loss are available from the specialty catalogues listed in the Resources section, and many are available commercially as well.

Although Chapter 3 provides more information about getting around in the world outside your home, in this chapter Mrs. Ringgold mentions the use of the collapsible cane to identify her as visually impaired—in the United States the symbol for persons with vision loss is a white cane with red tip—and to help her cross streets. It is very important, however, to obtain training in the use of a cane and the proper precautions and skills from a professional known as an orientation and mobility (O&M) specialist before attempting walking in traffic. The organizations listed in the Resources section can refer you to agencies with O&M specialists.

✧ 3 ✧
The Outside World

Support from family and friends is a big morale booster, especially in the beginning. It can take many forms—encouragement, physical help ("Will you read me this telephone number?" "Are these socks green?" "I can't seem to open this box"), and comments ("Do you know you have a run in your left stocking?" "Let me get this stain off your lapel"), including this one, addressed to me: "Grandma, you're wearing a yellow shoe and a white one. Is that a new fashion?" Friends can also be helpful in your early stages of organizing and labeling items so you can find them, particularly if they follow your directions and identify objects and their colors for you.

Helpful Friends

It takes a while for a person recently blinded or visually impaired to discover the limitations of the new state. There will be trying, groping, succeeding, and failing, until the situation becomes more stable and a routine is established. For your friends, too, there is a period when they don't know what you can do and what is beyond your capability. They may be overzealous in some instances and utterly uncomprehending in others. How can they tell what is visible and what is just a blur to you? They will take your arm to help you step down a clearly marked curb or to walk along a smooth sidewalk, but they will let you stumble alone over the dips and hollows of a grass plot. They'll say, "I'm putting this away," not realizing that the word *this* is a visual one that has no meaning for you and that they should have said, "I'm putting this towel away."

Or they'll say, "All you have to do is put this pin in this little hole, see?" when you can see neither pin nor hole and have to feel them to know they exist. Some adjustment is needed on both sides. A thoughtful friend will let you do whatever you are able to, even though it is slow and frustrating and requires patience to watch, knowing that even a small action can be an achievement that gives you a sense of self-esteem and accomplishment. You will have to accept gracefully the well-meaning assistance given with such generosity and love. Dependence is a hard lesson to learn, especially for someone who has been living alone, and for an ex-driver.

But where would we be without our friends? The answer is: at home. Since driving is no longer possible, mobility is restricted to a very small radius, outside which help is needed. Daily life has to be organized differently. Instead of a dash for a forgotten loaf of bread or a quick trip to the bank, activities have to be clustered so the kindly neighbor does not have to be called on too often. Your friends say, "Call me when you need me." You've run out of toothpaste or stamps; you need a card for Aunt Mattie's 80th birthday. Are you going to bother your neighbor? Of course not. Next time you'll have to plan earlier, and the post office can be combined with the hardware store, drugstore, and music store.

Some friends are especially helpful. Instead of leaving the initiative to you, they will call and say, "I'm going to the grocery store. Can I get you something?" or "I have a few errands to do. Would you like to come with me?" or "I'll be going to town at ten o'clock. Can I come and pick you up?" or even "It's such a beautiful day; how about going out for a little ride?" Bless you, my friends. For at least two hours I will no longer be a pedestrian confined to a few neighborhood blocks.

When you are a woman, and even more when you are an old woman with white hair, many people will go out of their way to be polite to you. They will open doors for you and expect you to lead the way through doors, into stores, up stairs, out of buildings, and on narrow sidewalks. The only drawback for the low vision woman is that this common courtesy puts squarely on her shoulders, or rather on her feet, the responsibility for avoiding steps, thresholds, loose rugs, uneven textures, glass doors or partitions, muddy patches, telephone poles, hurrying pedestrians, slippery places, potholes, and puddles. If the sighted friend goes first, the low vision follower has only to watch the motions of the person ahead to tell where the pitfalls are and when to step up, down, or sideways. Macular degeneration makes us good followers, not good pioneers.

Walking

We live in an area with fairly good side-walks, and my shopping expeditions don't take me very far. I know most of the cracks in the pavement, the brick that sticks up, the high curb, and the sudden dip for wheelchairs and can walk quite comfortably and confidently. Not so in the beginning, when it was still quite an undertaking to go out walking by myself. Since I don't use a cane for walking, I learned to proceed cautiously and use my toes like antennae, probing what lay ahead. And even now, in unfamiliar terrain, I rely on them to give me advance notice of any hazards.

One particular situation is baffling—what is reality and what is shadow? One time I thought there was a big fire hose lying across the street. When I carefully inched my foot forward, my toes told me it was the shadow of a telephone pole. On another occasion, however, what I thought was a shadow proved to be a branch that had fallen across the side walk. Shadows are very treacherous, and one should be very cautious around them, even if one has a cane or other safe way of exploring them from afar. They might *not* be shadows.

Shopping and Errands

Some errands I can do by myself, such as going to the bank, the post office, or the cleaner's. But for shopping, when selection comes into play and size, price, color, or quantity may be important, another pair of eyes is needed. The shelves in a local supermarket are familiar to me. So I act like a hunting dog on point: I make straight for the peanut butter and stop until my escort catches up and can tell me which is creamy and which chunky. The same for napkins. Which are yellow, which are white? Which trash bags are 8-gallon size? How much are the strawberries? How many tea bags in the package?

Sometimes you'll need to enlist the help of a store employee to direct you or take you to the item you are looking for. If you don't wear eyeglasses (or even if you do) and walk fairly confidently, no one will realize your limitations if you don't ask for help or ask questions. This is a point I can't emphasize enough. It's fine to be independent, it's fine to tell yourself, "I can do it," but we can't escape the fact that we do have visual impairments, that there are things we cannot do, and that when they have to be done, we have to put our pride in our pockets and ask for help. People are usually glad to give assistance, and many will go out of their way to do so.

Signs and Notices

When you don't wear eyeglasses and can navigate, it doesn't occur to anyone that you cannot read. Such notices or signs as This Way Out, Watch Your Step, Restrooms,

To the Trains, No Admittance, Keep Off the Grass, or those giving store hours enter the consciousness of sighted people automatically, while to us they are undecipherable mysteries. The solution is to ask—ask again and again. You will get the answer and probably a question as well. "Do you have cataracts?" "Do you have glaucoma?" Once there was a variation. A woman, hearing my foreign accent, asked, "Can't you read English, or can't you read at all?"

Cash

In money matters, we have to trust the people we deal with to let us know how much they're handing us since we can't tell the difference among $1, $5, $10, and $20 bills. But once we know the value of a bill, we can fold it in such a way that we will recognize it. I fold a $20 bill in half lengthwise; the $10 bill in half in the other direction, and again in half, which makes it quarter-size. The $5 bill is folded in thirds, and the $1 bill is not folded at all. There are other methods of folding money, but I learned mine from a blind student and have since passed it on to a great many people, including foreigners who complain about the uniformity of our paper money— their bills show difference by size or texture and color.

Now for the coins. The young man from the state commission gave me pointers on those. The quarter has a serrated edge; so does the dime. This serves to distinguish them from the penny and the nickel, which have smooth edges.

When a cashier gives me change for a $20 bill, I ask what the bills are. Cashiers have always waited patiently until I have my money folded and put away. I have never been cheated. Once, when I handed over a $10 bill instead of a $1 bill (because I had not folded it), the cashier pointed out my mistake and handed back the bill. So don't hurry, take your time. Fold your bills before putting them away. If you don't, you will have trouble with your next purchase.

I find that people are very kind and patient when they realize you have an impairment, but that is probably because I live in a small town. It might be different in a big city.

Voting

You might think that not being able to read would affect your ability to exercise your rights as a citizen at voting time. Not so. At each polling place there is a person authorized to go into the voting booth with you, who will read the appropriate information to you so that you can push the lever or make your mark for the candidate of your choice. You can also vote by absentee ballot.

Handicapped Parking

If you are legally blind, in many states the department of motor vehicles will issue you a cardboard permit you can carry with you and use in any vehicle in which you are a passenger. Place it on the driver's side behind the windshield, and the car in which you are traveling will be able to park in any space reserved for disabled people. Don't forget to retrieve the permit at the end of the ride; it is your personal card and does not go with any special vehicle. The convenience is much appreciated by the friends who offer to drive you since they will be able to park in any "handicapped" space. If the driving is done mostly in a car you own, the department of motor vehicles will sell you a special license plate with a handicapped logo on it, which will confer the same privilege.

Travel

Recently I embarked on a new venture and assumed a role new to me: that of a visually impaired traveler. I suppose that bus or train travel offers no great difficulty to a person with macular degeneration, provided his or her destination is the end of the line and someone awaits the passenger's arrival. If one's stop is at an intermediate point, the kindness of the driver or the loud voice of the conductor may be an important factor in one's feelings of confidence and security. Should a change of vehicle be necessary, one may have to rely somewhat on the good will and competence of a fellow traveler or some official. My experience has been with air travel. Because of sickness in the family, travel had been out of the question for a long time. Now, at age 86, I was setting out on a trip to Europe. By then I had been without central vision for seven years. Not knowing how well I could manage by myself, I asked my granddaughter to accompany me. Her main activities on my behalf were to have the luggage checked, which I could have done; to locate the ladies' room in the terminal, which I could not have done; and to describe the contents of my plate at dinnertime. The airline provided a wheelchair on departure and arrival; an attendant whisked us through lines for passports and customs and straight to the line of waiting taxis. Further travel was done with family and friends. My granddaughter had to return a week before I did, so I was on my own on the way back. Again, a wheelchair at departure and arrival, and a very enjoyable trip.

The success of this first venture encouraged me, at 87, again by myself, to undertake a short domestic trip and a longer European one, each involving a change of planes. The airlines had been alerted that I would need help; there were wheelchairs waiting, and attendants to take me from one airline to the other. Since I could not read a single sign, place and time of departure, flight number, or gate number, I needed assistance, which was given pleasantly and efficiently. The weeks away from home were spent with friends and family. The experience was an invigorating one. It enriched my sedentary life considerably, but most of all it created new possibilities and a more optimistic attitude toward the limitations imposed by my vision loss.

From My Perspective

Did you recognize some of your problems in my descriptions? Your own solutions may be better than mine, but I hope some of my suggestions may be of help to you. Considering it from every angle, coping with macular degeneration is not an easy task. Patience and ingenuity will eliminate a few of the practical problems; its main difficulties, however, will remain with us. Only our general attitude can decide to what extent they will dominate our lives. The best help we can receive is within ourselves and within easy reach—a healthy dose of determination, tempered by a lavish sprinkling of good humor.

✦ Living with Macular ✦ Degeneration Today

Since the passage of the Americans with Disabilities Act (ADA) in 1990, just before Mrs. Ringgold wrote her book, the world outside the home has become somewhat more accessible to people with low vision or other disabilities, as public facilities have made efforts to accommodate their needs in response to the law's mandates. The support of family and friends, however, is just as important as ever. As Esther Smith suggests, "Try to be independent, but don't be afraid to ask for help. People often want to help, but don't know what to do." You need to explain exactly what you want your friend to do and what you can do on your own.

When you are walking in the community with friends and family, they can use a technique known as "sighted guide," so that you do not have to try to follow someone else using sight. The visually impaired person takes the sighted guide's arm just above the elbow, and the companion walks about half a step in front to guide the person properly. More information and a video on sighted guide and other techniques for getting around safely are available on the Senior Site web page, www.afb.org/seniorsite. As noted in Chapter 2, assistance is also available from a person known as an orientation and mobility (O&M) specialist, who can help you learn to use a white cane to avoid pitfalls in your walking path.

Some of the products and devices mentioned in Chapter 2, such as portable electronic magnifiers and other optical low vision devices, can be a big help when shopping and doing errands. There are even special divided wallets available for keeping the different denominations of bills separate after they are folded in different ways. Also, paratransit systems or Access-a-Ride services are available in more and more locations that can help you get around independently. (The Eldercare service locator, described in the Resources section, can help you find these services in a particular area.) An O&M specialist can also give training on using public transportation.

Among the other changes brought about by the Americans with Disabilities Act and the increasing awareness of the needs of people with disabilities, talking ATMs (automated teller machines) are now available at many banks. These ATMs provide audible instructions so that persons who cannot read an ATM screen can independently use the machine. To guard your privacy, there is either a telephone handset to listen through or a standard headphone jack on the face of the machine where you can plug in earphones. Also, voting machines adapted to be independently usable by people with visual impairments and other disabilities are now mandated by the Help America Vote Act. At least one accessible voting machine is supposed to be available in each polling place. Next time you vote, ask to use an accessible machine.

Traveling by air may be more complicated today than it was for Ms. Ringgold, but that does not need to be a deterrent to flying. Esther Smith offers a number of travel tips that work for her:

• Don't be embarrassed to ask for help.

- Be sure to identify yourself ahead of time as having a visual impairment.

- Memorize your identification numbers, charge card numbers, passport number, and bank number. Or you may want to set up a system to get to them easily should you lose your wallet.

- You can ask the airline to provide an escort to help you get to and from the plane easily and efficiently, and you can request a wheelchair if you need one.

- When you book your reservations, ask for the security guidelines and how much time you need to allow for clearing these requirements.

- You may want to ask for assistance when going through security lines to help you retrieve all your belongings after they go through the X-ray machine, especially small items placed in tubs.

Finally, Esther notes, "Add patience to the mix. Your determination can give you the confidence to try other things. For me personally, an important point is to act as a role model for my family and other people living with macular degeneration. Remember, determination, confidence, patience, and humor will get you everywhere."

Resources

As demonstrated throughout *Out of the Corner of My Eye*, people with macular degeneration and other vision conditions can continue to live independent, productive lives. Services, assistance, and information for people who have experienced vision loss or who are blind or visually impaired are available from a great number of sources. This Resources section offers a sample of resources available in the three main areas of Information on Macular Degeneration and Visual Impairment, Resources for Independent Living, and Resources for Recreation. There is also a list of books and videos for additional information. If you don't find a specific source listed that meets your needs or has the answers to your questions, one of the organizations listed in the first section should be able to refer you to a source that does.

All states have departments of rehabilitation or agencies for the blind that can provide information on available services and agencies for people with vision loss. Listings for these agencies can be found in the state and county government sections of the local telephone directory or online on the state or local government web site. The American Foundation for the Blind (AFB) publishes a comprehensive list of vision-related services, the *AFB Directory of Services for Blind and Visually Impaired Persons in the United States and Canada*, which is available in some libraries and can also be accessed online at www.afb .org/directory or through AFB's Senior Site web page at www.afb.org/seniorsite. In addition, each state has an agency, department, or office responsible for state programs for older people funded by the Older Americans Act, and each county or group of counties has an Area Agency on Aging (AAA) that will know about the availability of such programs as home-delivered meals, door-to-door transportation and escort services, and other services for elderly persons. To find your local Area Agency on Aging, call (800) 677-1116 or go to www.eldercare.gov on the Internet.

Special vision examinations, known as low vision evaluations, are essential for helping people determine how to use their remaining vision to maximum advantage. These evaluations are available from low vision services, which can be found in such settings as hospitals, departments of ophthalmology at medical schools, and agencies for blind and visually impaired persons, as well as from some private practitioners. State and local agencies for persons who are blind or visually impaired can provide further information on sources of low vision services, as can AFB's information line and *Directory of Services.*

One section of this listing is devoted to sources of products and information that can help with everyday activities and maintaining an active and independent life. Information and assistance are also available in regard to activities that might be characterized as recreational, including reading, listening to the radio, enjoying television and movies, and other activities. For example, the National Library Service (NLS) for the Blind and Physically Handicapped of the Library of Congress offers recorded and braille books free of charge through a network of regional and subregional libraries across the country; information on how to enroll in this program can be obtained from NLS, which is listed in this resource section, or from local libraries. Other publishers offer recorded books or magazines, and today electronic books in a variety of formats are available from online services. A great variety of large-print books and audiocassettes are also available commercially. A number of publishers and organizations that provide these books are listed here.

Additional information about visual impairment and living with visual impairment can be obtained from a large variety of resources. Many organizations on the national, state, and local levels provide information, assistance, and referrals; operate toll-free hotlines; and publish materials that are valuable sources of information for visually impaired people and their families. A great deal of information and links to other resources can be found on AFB's Senior Site web site for older adults with vision loss, www.afb.org/seniorsite, and by contacting the AFB Center on Vision Loss as well as AFB's toll-free information line (see AFB's listing later in the Information section). Many of the other national organizations listed in this section can also be contacted for general information about visual impairment or for specific information about a particular eye condition and relevant services. As already noted, a complete listing of local, state, and national agencies and organizations serving people who are blind or visually impaired is included in the *AFB Directory of Services for Blind and Visually Impaired Persons in the United States and Canada*, or at www.afb.org.

Information on Macular Degeneration and Visual Impairment

Organizations listed in this section provide general information about visual impairment and blindness, macular degeneration, and services for older people, as well as referrals for additional information and services.

Administration on Aging
U.S. Department of Health and Human
  Services
One Massachusetts Avenue
Washington, DC 20201
(202) 619-0724; (800) 677-1116 (Eldercare
  Locator)
E-mail: aoainfo@aoa.hhs.gov
www.aoa.gov
www.eldercare.gov

Administers programs for older people
funded under the Older Americans Act of
1965. It develops programs to promote
the economic welfare and personal independence of older people and provides
funds, advice, and assistance to promote
the development of state-administered,
community-based social services for older
people. Its Eldercare Locator connects
older Americans and their caregivers with
sources of information on senior services
and links those who need assistance with
state and local Area Agencies on Aging

and community-based organizations that serve older adults and their caregivers.

American Academy of Ophthalmology

P.O. Box 7424
San Francisco, CA 94120-7424
(415) 561-8500
Fax: (415) 561-8533
E-mail: eca@aao.org (Eye Care America); customer_service@aao.org (Customer Service)
www.aao.org

As a professional membership association for eye care physicians, works to ensure that the public can obtain the best possible eye care. Provides information on eye health for consumers and referrals to member physicians.

American Foundation for the Blind

11 Penn Plaza, Suite 300
New York, NY 10001
(800) 232-5463 or (212) 502-7600

E-mail: afbinfo@afb.net (general information); seniorsite@afb.net (Senior Site)
www.afb.org
www.afb.org/seniorsite

Provides services to and serves as an information clearinghouse for people who are blind or visually impaired and their families, professionals, organizations, schools, and corporations. Provides information on many aspects of visual impairment, including aging and vision loss through fact sheets and its web sites, including Senior Site. Stimulates research and mounts program initiatives to improve services to blind and visually impaired people. Publishes a wide variety of professional, reference, and consumer books and videos; a journal; an online magazine, *AccessWorld: Technology and People Who Are Blind or Visually Impaired*; and the *AFB Directory of Services for Blind and Visually Impaired Persons in the United States and Canada*. AFB maintains offices across the country as well as a governmental relations office in Washington, DC, and the AFB Center on Vision Loss, a national demonstration center that offers people with vision loss a chance to try out helpful devices and technologies and shows them what they can do in their own living environments to enhance independence and safety.

AFB Center on Vision Loss
11030 Ables Lane
Dallas, TX 75229
(214) 352-7222
E-mail: dallas@afb.net

American Macular Degeneration Foundation
P.O. Box 515
Northampton, MA 01061-0515
(413) 268-7660
E-mail: amdf@macular.org
www.macular.org

Works for the prevention, treatment, and cure of macular degeneration by raising funds, educating the public and supporting scientific research.

American Optometric Association
243 North Lindbergh Boulevard
St. Louis, MO 63141
(800) 365-2219 or (314) 991-4100
Fax: (314) 991-4101
www.aoanet.org

Provides information on visual conditions, eye diseases, and low vision; consumer guides for eye care; and referrals to optometrists.

American Retina Foundation
8833 Perimeter Park Boulevard, Suite 301
Jacksonville, FL 32216
(904) 998-0356
www.americanretina.org
www.savingvision.org

An organization formed by the American Society of Retina Specialists, promotes public awareness, continuing medical education, research, and treatment of retinal diseases. Its online web project, www.savingvision.org, features an interactive slide presentation, brochure, and patient resources concerning age-related macular degeneration and other retinal diseases.

American Society of Retina Specialists
PMB #A
2485 Notre Dame Boulevard, Suite 370
Chico, CA 95928
(530) 566-9181
Fax: (530) 566-9192
E-mail:cordie@asrs.org
www.asrs.org

As a professional organization of vitreoretinal specialists, provides referrals to retinal specialists all over the world through its web site.

Associates for World Action in Education & Rehabilitation (AWARE)
P.O. Box 96
Mohegan Lake, NY 10547
(914) 528-5120
E-mail: info@visionaware.org
www.visionaware.org

Promotes self-help vision rehabilitation hints and adaptive techniques and disseminates information on services and independent living resources to individuals with recent vision loss, their family members, and those who work with them, through its web site VisionAWARE Self Help for Vision Loss, online newsletter *Are You Aware*, publications, and Low Vision Forum.

Association for Macular Diseases
210 East 64th Street
New York, NY 10021
(212) 605-3719
Fax: (212) 605-3795

E-mail: association@retinal-research.org
www.macula.org/association/about.html

Acts as a nationwide support group for
individuals and their families endeavoring
to adjust to the changes brought about
by macular disease. It publishes a quar-
terly newsletter, maintains a hotline for its
members, and conducts nationwide educational seminars for the public on macular
degeneration.

Blinded Veterans Association
477 H Street, N.W.
Washington, DC 20001-2694
(800) 669-7079 or (202) 371-8880
E-mail: bva@bva.org
www.bva.org

Provides support and assistance to blind
veterans to enable them to take advantage of rehabilitation and vocational training benefits, job placement services, and

other aid from federal, state, and local resources.

The Foundation Fighting Blindness
11435 Cronhill Drive
Owings Mills, MD 21117-2220
(800) 683-5555 or (410) 568-0150
TDD/TTY: (800) 683-5551 or
  (410) 363-7139
E-mail: info@fightblindness.org
www.blindness.org

Funds and supports research to provide preventions, treatments and cures for people affected by macular degeneration, retinitis pigmentosa, Usher syndrome, and the entire spectrum of retinal degenerative diseases. Provides information to increase knowledge and awareness of retinal de-generative diseases. Has over 30 volun-teer-led groups across the United States to raise funds, increase public awareness, and provide support to their communities.

Hadley School for the Blind
700 Elm Street
Winnetka, IL 60093
(800) 323-4238 or (847) 446-8111
TDD/TTY: (847) 441-8111
Fax: (847) 446-9916
E-mail: info@hadley.edu
www.hadley.edu

Offers correspondence courses in braille
and on cassette for legally blind persons.
Courses include special programs on independent living for elderly blind and visually
impaired persons.

Lighthouse International
111 East 59th Street
New York, NY 10022-1202
(800) 829-0500 or (212) 821-9200
TDD/TTY: (212) 821-9713
Fax: (212) 821-9707
E-mail: info@lighthouse.org
www.lighthouse.org

Works to overcome visual impairment for people of all ages through worldwide leadership in rehabilitation services, education, research, and advocacy. Provides rehabilitation services, including training in adaptive living skills and computer skills for seniors. Publishes the newsletter *Aging & Vision* and other publications on age-related vision loss for both professional and lay audiences. Maintains a catalog of independent living products.

Macular Degeneration Foundation
P.O. Box 531313
Henderson, NV 89053
(888) 633-3937
Fax: 702-450-3396
E-mail: eyesight@eyesight.org
www.eyesight.org

A medical research and educational foundation that supports research to inhibit the progression of macular degeneration and restore vision. Publishes *The Magnifier* newsletter.

Macular Degeneration Partnership
8733 Beverly Boulevard, Suite 201
Los Angeles, CA 90048
(888) 430-9898
Fax: (310) 623-1937
www.AMD.org

A coalition of patients and families, researchers, clinicians, industry partners and leaders in the fields of vision and aging collaborating to disseminate information about age-related macular degeneration, provide support to patients, and marshal resources for a cure. Maintains a Help Center on the Internet that provides users with links to web sites for health, aging, and low vision information, along with tools and other related resources. Also maintains a toll-free telephone line.

National Association for Visually Handicapped
22 West 21st Street
New York, NY 10010
(212) 889-3141 or (212) 255-2804
Fax: (212) 727-2931
E-mail: navh@navh.org
www.navh.org

507 Polk Street, Suite 420
San Francisco, CA 94102
(415) 775-6284
Fax: (415) 346-9593
E-mail: staffca@navh.org

Provides information and referral for people with low vision on large-print books, low vision devices, medical advances and updates, craft materials and projects, resource guides, and religious materials. Sells low vision products and devices. Maintains a large-print mail-order library. Promotes public awareness of low vision.

National Eye Care Project
Eye Care America
P.O. Box 429098
San Francisco, CA 94142-9098
(800) 222-3937 (Senior Eye Care Program)
www.eyecareamerica.org

Provides medical and surgical eye care for persons over 65 years of age at no out-of-pocket cost through a network of volunteer ophthalmologists around the country. Provides literature on eye diseases and procedures.

National Eye Institute
Building 31, Room 6A32
31 Center Drive, MSC 2510
Bethesda, MD 20892-2510
(301) 496-5248
Fax: (301) 402-1065
E-mail: 2020@nei.nih.gov
www.nei.nih.gov

Established by Congress in 1968 to protect and prolong the vision of the American people, conducts and supports research that helps prevent and treat eye diseases and other disorders of vision. Provides information on advances in eye disease research and about clinical trials.

Prevent Blindness America
211 West Wacker Drive, Suite 1700
Chicago, IL 60606
(800) 331-2020 or (312) 363-6001
Fax: (312) 363-6052
E-mail: info@preventblindness.org
www.preventblindness.org

Conducts a program of public and professional education, research, and industrial and community services to prevent blindness. Promotes local glaucoma screening programs, vision testing, and eye safety and dissemination of information on low vision devices and clinics; and maintains a network of state affiliates.

Social Security Administration
6401 Security Boulevard
Baltimore, MD 21235
(800) 772-1213
TDD/TTY: (800) 325-0778

Oversees old age, survivors, and disability insurance programs under the provisions of the Social Security Act, including the Supplemental Security Income (SSI) program for aged, blind, and disabled persons. Maintains a network of offices across the country and publishes a variety of materials on Social Security benefits.

U.S. Department of Veterans Affairs
Blind Rehabilitation Service
810 Vermont Avenue, NW
Washington, DC 20420
(888) 442-4551 or (202) 273-8481
Fax: (202) 273-7603
E-mail: wandawashington@va.gov
www1.va.gov/blindrehab

Oversees programs for visually impaired veterans through a network of rehabilitation centers, clinics, and field staff throughout the country. Services include orientation and mobility, living skills, communication skills, activities of daily living, manual skills, computer access training, physical conditioning, recreation, adjustment to blindness, family counseling, and group meetings. Also supplies needed devices, appliances, and equipment.

Resources for Independent Living

Many specialized products, some of which are referred to in this book, are available to help people with vision loss carry out their everyday activities more easily. These are often most readily obtained through specialty catalogs, a number of which are listed here, along with some sources of devices that help with reading prescription labels.

✧ Catalogs and Sources of Products

The companies listed in this section sell a wide variety of specialized products that help people with visual impairments and other disabilities carry out everyday activities. The types of products in each catalog are indicated in the listing.

Ableware/Maddak

661 Route 23 South
Wayne, NJ 07470
(973) 628-7600
Fax: (973) 305-0841
E-mail: custservice@maddak.com
http://service.maddak.com

Designs and manufactures assistive devices for activities of daily living. Offers adapted games, adapted scissors, eating utensils and tableware, enlarged grips, nonskid table mats, and writing devices.

Adaptive Solutions

301 Azalea Road, Suite 102
P.O. Box 191087
Mobile, AL 33619-1087
(800) 299 3045 or (251) 666-3045
Fax: (251) 660-1788
www.talksight.com

Sells assistive technology products for persons who are blind or visually impaired.

Ambutech

34 DeBaets Street
Winnipeg, MB R2J 3S9
Canada
(800) 561 3340 or (204) 663-3340
Fax: (800) 267-5059
E-mail: orders@ambutech.com
www.ambutech.com

Sells a wide range of mobility equipment.

American Printing House for the Blind

1839 Frankfort Avenue

P.O. Box 6085
Louisville, KY 40206-0085
(800) 223-1839 or (502) 895-2405
Fax: (502) 899-2274
E-mail: info@aph.org
www.aph.org

Distributes braille products, books, and supplies; large-print books; computer software and access products; labeling and marking products; lighting; low vision devices; mobility devices; personal care products; recreation and leisure products; talking products; and writing and reading devices.

Beyond Sight
5650 South Windermere Street
Littleton, CO 80120
(303) 795-6455
Fax: (303) 795-6425
E-mail: jim@beyondsight.com (sales);
   support@beyondsight.com (support)
www.beyondsight.com

Distributes a large variety of products, such as lamps and bulbs, writing aids, kitchen aids, clocks, and games, for people with low vision.

Clotilde
P.O. Box 7500
Big Sandy, TX 75755-7500
(800) 545-4002
E-mail: customer_service@clotilde.com
www.clotilde.com

Sells sewing notions, needle threaders, and regular and adaptive sewing supplies.

Howe Press
Perkins School for the Blind
175 North Beacon Street
Watertown, MA 02172
(617) 972-7308
E-mail: HowePress@Perkins.org

Manufactures and sells materials and equipment for reproducing materials in braille, including the Perkins Brailler, slates and styli, handwriting aids, braille games and paper, and drawing supplies.

Independent Living Aids
200 Robbins Lane
Jericho, NY 11753
(800) 537-2118 or (516) 937-1848
Fax: (516) 937-3906
E-mail: can-do@independentliving.com
www.independentliving.com

Distributes braille products and supplies, adapted clocks and watches, computer software and access products, diabetes management products, kitchen and house-keeping items, labeling and marking products, lighting, low vision devices, mobility devices, personal care products, recreation and leisure products, talking products, telephones and accessories, and writing and reading devices.

The Low Vision Store
2200 University Avenue, Suite 180
St. Paul, MN 55114
(800) 871-8780
E-mail: lowvisionstore@yahoo.com
www.thelowvisionstore.com

Distributes a variety of household and personal products such as talking clocks, large print appointment books, sewing supplies, lamps, and large-button telephones.

LS&S Group
P.O. Box 673
Northbrook, IL 60065
(800) 468-4789 or (847) 498-9777
TDD/TTY: (866) 317-8533
Fax: (847) 498-1482
E-mail: info@lssproducts.com
www.lssgroup.com

Distributes braille products and supplies, adapted clocks and watches, computer software and access products, diabetes management products, kitchen and house-keeping items, labeling and marking products, lighting, low vision devices, mobility devices, personal care products, recreation and leisure products, talking products, telephones and accessories, and writing and reading devices.

Maxi-Aids
42 Executive Boulevard
Farmingdale, NY 11735
(800) 522-6294 or (631) 752-0689
TDD/TTY: (800) 281-3555
Fax: (631) 752-0689
E-mail: sales@maxiaids.com
www.maxiaids.com

Distributes braille products and supplies, adapted clocks and watches, computer software and access products, diabetes management products, kitchen and house-keeping items, labeling and marking products, lighting, low vision devices, mobility devices, personal care products, recreation and leisure products, talking products, telephones and accessories, and writing and reading devices.

Mons International
6595 Roswell Road #224
Atlanta, GA 30328
(800) 541-7903 or (770) 551-8460
Fax: (770) 551-8455
E-mail: salesinfo@magnifiers.com (sales)
support@magnifiers.com (support)
www.magnifiers.com

Offers low vision products, including CCTVs, telescopes, and binoculars.

ShopLowVision
3030 Enterprise Court, Suite D
Vista, CA 92081-8358
(800) 826-4200
Fax: (800) 368-4111
www.shoplowvision.com

Offers a complete assortment of daily living aids and electronic magnification products, including magnifiers, special low vision reading glasses, microscopic low vision aids, and telescopic low vision aids.

✧ Talking Prescription Labels

Reading prescription labels can be made easier by using one of the systems listed here that can read aloud an electronic label on the medicine container.

Talking Prescription Labels
En-Vision America
1845 W. Hovey Avenue
(800) 890-1180 or (309) 452-3088
Fax: (309) 452-3643
E-mail: envision@envisionamerica.com
www.envisionamerica.com

Distributes ScripTalk, a portable, hand-held audio system that reads prescriptions aloud.

Talking Rx
P.O. Box 649
Southington, CT 06489
(888) 798-2557
www.talkingrx.com
E-mail: info@talkingrx.com

Distributes Talking Rx, an audio system that reads prescription labels aloud.

Resources for Recreation

✧ Reading

The sources listed here provide reading materials in alternate formats, including large-print, braille, or audio formats. See also the section Products for Independent Living in this appendix for specific products that can help with reading, as well as additional large-print reading materials, including cookbooks. For further reading resources, including electronic texts, consult information and fact sheets from the National Library Service (listed in this section).

Betty Crocker
P.O. Box 9452
Minneapolis, MN 55440
(800) 446-1898
Fax: (763) 764-8330

Offers popular recipes using Betty Crocker products. The Betty Crocker cookbook is available on computer disk for $35.00. Recipes in large print on 9" x 12" cards are free.

Books Aloud
150 E. San Fernando Street
San Jose, CA 95112-3580
(408) 808-2613
Fax: (408) 808-4625
E-mail: info@booksaloud.org
www.booksaloud.org

Offers "Reading by Listening" program, which provides a wide variety of recorded reading material free of charge to eligible individuals.

Choice Magazine Listening
85 Channel Drive
Port Washington, NY 11050
(888) 724-6423 or (516) 883-8280
Fax: (516) 944-6849
E-mail: choicemag@aol.com
www.choicemagazinelistening.org

Distributes a free monthly audio anthology of current articles chosen from over 100 leading magazines through regional libraries. Also available through individual subscription.

Doubleday Large Print Home Library
1225 South Market Street
Mechanicsburg, PA 17055
E-mail: service@doubledaylargeprint.com
www.doubledaylargeprint.com

Offers a large-print Book-of-the-Month Club.

Hansen House Music
Golden Music Big Note Songs
1820 West Avenue
Miami Beach, FL 33139
(305) 532-5461
Fax: (305) 672-8729
E-mail: info@hansenhousemusic.com
www.hansenhousemusic.com

Sells a wide selection of music books. Music notes are 1/2 inch across with the name of the note written inside the note. A free catalog is available.

Matilda Ziegler Magazine for the Blind
80 Eighth Avenue, Room 1304
New York, NY 10011
(212) 242-0263
Fax: (212) 633-1601
E-mail: blind@verizon.net
www.zieglermag.org

Free monthly general-interest periodical published in braille and on audiocassette.

National Library Service for the Blind and Physically Handicapped

Library of Congress
1291 Taylor Street, NW
Washington, DC 20542
(800) 424-8567 or (202) 707-5100
Fax: (202) 707-0712
TDD/TTY: (202) 707-0744
E-mail: nls@loc.gov
www.loc.gov/nls

Offers a free library service for people who are unable to read standard print materials because of a visual or physical impairment. Provides recorded Talking Books and magazines and braille publications to eligible borrowers by postage-free mail and through a network of cooperative libraries. Also distributes Talking Book machines.

New York Times Large-Type Weekly

609 Greenwich Street, 6th Floor
New York, NY 10014
(800) 631-2580 or (212) 905-3391

Fax: (212) 905-3436
E-mail: barber@nytimes.com
http://nytimes.com

Publishes a weekly news summary from the *New York Times* in 16 point print.

Reader's Digest Partners for Sight Foundation
Reader's Digest Road
Pleasantville, NY 10570
E-mail: PartnersForSight@rd.com
www.rd.com/partnersforsight/index.jsp

Publishes *Reader's Digest Large Print for Easier Reading.*

Recording for the Blind & Dyslexic
20 Roszel Road
Princeton, NJ 08540
(866) 732-3585 or (609) 452-0606
Fax: (609) 520-7990
E-mail: custserv@rfbd
www.rfbd.org

Lends recorded audiobooks on CD at no charge to anyone with a documented disability that makes reading standard print difficult or impossible and who becomes a member.

Thorndike Press
295 Kennedy Memorial Drive
Waterville, ME 04901
(800) 223-1244
Fax: (800) 558-4676
E-mail: printorders@thomson.com
www.gale.com/thorndike

One of the largest publishers of large-print books, Thorndike Press also distributes large-print books from other publishers.

✧ Electronic Texts

This listing provides a sample of web sites that offer books and other texts in a wide variety of electronic formats. Some are available free of charge; others have a variety of payment options. For a comprehensive list of electronic text resources, contact the National Library Service or see their fact sheet at http://lcweb.loc.gov/nls/reference/factsheets/etexts.html.

Accessible Book Collection
www.accessiblebookcollection.org
12847 Point Pleasant Drive
Fairfax, VA 22033
(703) 631-1585
Fax: (775) 256-2556
E-mail: customerservice@accessiblebook-
    collection.org

Audible.com
www.audible.com
One Washington Park
Newark, NJ 07102
(888) 283-5051 or (973) 820-0400

Bartleby.com
www.bartleby.com
E-mail: bartlebycom@aol.com

Bookshare.org
www.bookshare.org/web/Welcome.html
480 California Avenue, Suite 201
Palo Alto, CA 94306
(650) 475-5440
Fax: (650) 475-1066
E-mail: info@bookshare.org

ClassicReader.com
www.classicreader.com/

eBooks.com
http://ebooks.com//
120 Mount Vernon Street
Boston, MA 02108

Fictionwise
www.fictionwise.com
(973) 701-6771

4Literature
www.4literature.net
E-mail: jaret.wilson@javatar.net

netLibrary

www.netlibrary.com
4888 Pearl East Circle, Suite 103
Boulder, CO 80301
(800) 413-4557
(800) 848-5800 (technical/customer
   support)
E-mail: info@netlibrary.com

Project Gutenberg

www.gutenberg.org
809 North 1500 West
Salt lake City, UT 84116
E-mail: help@pglaf.org

✧ Radio and Telephone Reading Services

Radio information or reading services around the country broadcast parts or entire issues of local newspapers every day. Other services allow listeners to call in by telephone to listen to newspapers being read. Information on these services is available from the organizations listed here.

International Association of Audio Information Services
c/o The National Broadcast Reading
  Service
1090 Don Mills Road, #303
Toronto, ON M3C 3R6
(800) 280-5325
http://www.iaais.org/

As an international organization of radio reading services, connects listeners with services in their area that provide audio access to information for people who are print disabled (blind, visually impaired, learning disabled, or physically disabled), including news, feature stories, sports, advertisements, and other special programs.

InTouch Networks
15 West 65th Street
New York, NY 10023
(212) 769-6270
Fax: (917) 386-9811

E-mail: intouchinfo@jgb.org
http://66.40.142.226/InTouch/default.asp

Provides international programming services for local radio reading services for people who are blind or visually impaired. Offers closed-circuit radio broadcasts of national and local newspapers and magazines.

NFB-Newsline

National Federation of the Blind
1800 Johnson Street
Baltimore, MD 21230-4998
866-504-7300
www.nfb.org/nfb/Newspapers_by_Phone
  .asp

Provides 24-hour access by toll-free telephone call to over 200 newspapers from across the country, as well as magazines, television listings and other information, for people who cannot read conventional newsprint due to a physical disability.

✧ Video Description

Some television programs and films on videotape are available in video-described versions in which explanations and descriptions of the visual elements are inserted on the sound track without interfering with the sounds and dialogue that are part of the program. For some television programs, these descriptions can be heard on a Secondary Audio Program (SAP), a separate audio channel available on most stereo televisions sold in the United States. Programs are available on many public broadcasting and cable stations, and video-described movies can be purchased or borrowed from some libraries and video stores. Many movie theaters are also now screening films that are described. The following organizations offer additional information.

Descriptive Video Service
Media Access Group at WGBH
125 Western Avenue

Boston, MA 02134
(617) 300-3600 (Voice/TDD);
 (800) 333-1203 (Pre-recorded
 information line)
Fax: (617) 300-1020
E-mail: access@wgbh.org
www.wgbh.org/access

Narrative Television Network
5840 South Memorial Drive, Suite 312
Tulsa, OK 74145
(918) 627-1000
Fax: (918) 627-4101
E-mail: narrative@aol.com
www.narrativeTV.com

Further Reading and Information

✧ From AFB Press

The following books and videos are available from AFB Press through American

Foundation for the Blind's web site at www.afb.org/store or by contacting AFB Press at (800) 232-3044 or at afborder@ abdintl.com. AFB books are available on cassette, ASCII disk, or online, as well as in print.

Books

Aging and Vision Loss: A Handbook for Families, by Alberta L. Orr and Priscilla Rogers (2006)

Written for the adult children of older people with vision loss, this handbook contains a wealth of information about how to manage independently, as well as how to obtain services and the emotional impact of losing vision later in life.

Making Life More Livable: Simple Adaptations for Living at Home after Vision Loss, revised by Maureen A. Duffy (2002)

A guide for adults experiencing vision loss and their family and friends. Includes practical tips with numerous photographs that show how people who are visually impaired can continue living independent, productive lives at home on their own. Useful general guidelines and room-by-room specifics provide simple and effective solutions for making homes accessible and everyday activities doable for individuals with visual impairments.

Videos
Aging and Vision: Declaration of Independence (1984)

Five profiles of individuals who have successfully coped with visual impairment in their later years. Offers practical suggestions on how to live independent, active, and satisfying lives.

Profiles in Aging and Vision, by Alberta L. Orr (1998)

An overview of the vision-related services available to older, visually impaired individuals, illustrated with interviews and personal accounts.

Brochures

Aging and Vision: Making the Most of Impaired Vision (1987)

Informative pamphlet on helping individuals who are elderly cope with visual impairment in real, practical ways. Offers helpful tips for improving lighting, decorating with contrasting colors, and using devices for independent living.

Consider Older Workers Who Are Visually Impaired

A brochure that explains positive reasons to hire older persons with visual impairments for employers as well as reasonable accommodations that make this feasible.

✧ Other Publications

Macular Degeneration: The Complete Guide to Saving Your Sight, by Lilas G. Mogk and Marja Mogk (New York: Ballantine Books, 2003).

The First Year: Age-Related Macular Degeneration: An Essential Guide for the Newly Diagnosed, by Daniel L. Roberts (New York: Marlowe & Co., 2006).

Living Well with Macular Degeneration: Practical Tips and Essential Information, by Bruce P. Rosenthal, O.D. and Kate Kelly (New York: New American Library, 2001).

About the Author

Nicolette Pernot Ringgold, a retired college professor and homemaker who lived in Williamsburg, Virginia, was born in Paris, France, in 1903. A graduate of the University of Paris, she taught at the Alliance Française and the Institute de Phonétique of the Sorbonne before coming to the United States, where she taught at Middlebury College, Wellesley College, and the College of William and Mary. She was the author of several manuals and various articles on phonetics and co-authored *Add Color to Your French* with her husband, Gordon B. Ringgold. They had two sons and a number of grandchildren and great-grandchildren.

At age 79 Mrs. Ringgold lost her central vision after developing macular degeneration, and some 15 years later wrote *Out of the Corner of My Eye* about her experiences in living with vision loss. Mrs. Ringgold died in 2003 at the age of 99.